BOMBARDIER

A dream with
international reach

BOMBARDIER

A dream with international reach

© Bombardier Inc., 1992
800 René-Lévesque Blvd. West
Montréal, Québec
Canada H3B 1Y8

Copyright Registration: 3rd quarter 1992
Bibliothèque nationale du Québec
ISBN 2-921393-09-3

Printed in Canada

CONTENTS

A dream with international reach

The album entitled "A dream with international reach" is yet another way of commemorating the half century that has passed since L'Auto-Neige Bombardier Limitée came into being on July 10, 1942. It is meant as both a tribute to Joseph-Armand Bombardier, who had a dream and succeeded in making it come true, and an account of our company's technical, industrial and commercial achievements over the last 50 years.

From the time the B7* tracked vehicle was invented, put into production and brought to market, to today's large-scale projects designed to ensure our participation in the global economy, our company has travelled far and erected many milestones along the way: the 1959 launch of the Ski-Doo* snowmobile, the invention that gave Joseph-Armand Bombardier a claim to fame; the 1969 acquisition of Austrian manufacturer Rotax, the first step of industrial expansion in Europe; the diversification into rail transit equipment in 1974 with the Montréal subway car contract; the key order for New York City subway cars in 1982; the diversification into aerospace through the 1986 acquisition of Canadair; and national and international expansion with the addition of BN, Shorts, ANF-Industrie, Bombardier Prorail, Learjet, UTDC, de Havilland and Concarril.

To the readers who have shared in the Company's recent past, these pages will bring, I hope, the same enjoyment as would a family album. To others, they should give a more complete, and perhaps more intimate, understanding of Bombardier's growth.

Laurent Beaudoin,
Chairman and Chief Executive Officer,
BOMBARDIER INC.

September 1992

Joseph-Armand Bombardier: Inventive genius and entrepreneurial spirit

The man who created L'Auto-Neige Bombardier Limitée in 1942 was born in 1907 near the village of Valcourt, in Québec's Eastern Townships.

As a child, Joseph-Armand Bombardier was fascinated with machinery. He nurtured the dream of inventing a motorized vehicle that could travel on snow-covered roads and relieve people in rural and remote areas from the isolation of winter.

At the age of 19, he set up a garage in Valcourt and practised his trade as a mechanic. Over the next 10 years he devoted most of his spare time to research and experimentation, showing a rare degree of drive and determination.

From 1926 to 1935, he developed various prototype vehicles, ranging from light one- and two-seat models to much larger ones. Since the automobile engines available at the time did not entirely satisfy him, he began looking into the possibility of building his own. He also tried out many types of track.

In 1935, faced with the lack of suitable engines for smaller models, Joseph-Armand Bombardier made a decision to produce heavier vehicles that could accommodate several passengers. In the summer of 1936, he built a seven-passenger "snowmobile" for which he perfected a revolutionary rear-wheel drive and suspension system. He had finally resolved the problem of travelling over snow to his own satisfaction.

On December 21, 1936, the inventor submitted this snowmobile, named the B7, to Ottawa for his first patent. Within a short time he had sold 20 of these vehicles.

The approval of the B7 patent the following June crowned 10 years of hard work. It confirmed the inventive genius of Joseph-Armand Bombardier and opened the way to commercial production of the Bombardier snowmobile.

The next two decades would witness the establishment of a new company and its path to growth and prosperity.

Le Garage Bombardier, opened in 1926 in Valcourt,
in Québec's Eastern Townships.

*For the 1935 snowmobile model, the inventor designed a sprocket wheel
(a rubber-coated cogged wheel) and a rubber track system.
These two innovations represented a crucial turning point in his research.
The sprocket wheel was incorporated into the Company's logo in 1959
to highlight its importance.*

The Company produced about 150 B7 vehicles between 1937 and 1942.

L'Auto-Neige Bombardier: a promising start

Even though L'Auto-Neige Bombardier was only incorporated in 1942, a confident Joseph-Armand Bombardier decided to build and market his B7 snowmobile as early as 1937.

Thus the mechanic-turned-industrialist also became an entrepreneur. He put together a small team of workers, which he personally trained, and recruited several members of his family into the business. Juggling the tasks of president, head engineer and chief of production, he also supervised the creation of a sales network and marketing program to spread the word about his invention.

From 1937 onward, demand for the B7 never stopped growing. The vehicle met the needs of a large snowbound clientele consisting of country doctors and veterinarians, taxi and bus owners, hotel-keepers, merchants, foresters, electrical utilities and telephone companies.

To keep up with the demand, Joseph-Armand Bombardier had a modern factory built in 1940, with an annual capacity of 200 vehicles. A year later, he developed a second, bigger and more powerful snowmobile which he named the B12*.

But the prosperity that had been anticipated in the late 1930s did not materialize immediately. The onset of World War II in 1939 and Canada's introduction of the War Measures Act in 1941 jeopardized the Company's very existence. Restrictions imposed first on machine tools and energy consumption and then on motorized vehicles forced a drastic reduction in snowmobile production. Despite strong civilian demand, production decreased from 70 units in 1940-41 to only 27 units in 1941-42.

Like most other Canadian companies, L'Auto-Neige Bombardier joined in the war effort. Joseph-Armand Bombardier quickly realized that he would be in a better position to do business with the government if his company were to have a legal framework. He also felt that a more formal management structure would allow his closest colleagues to benefit from the Company's emerging prosperity.

L'Auto-Neige Bombardier Limitée was thus incorporated on July 10, 1942. Its head office was established at Valcourt, Québec, and its authorized share capital was set at 3,000 shares.

At the time, Joseph-Armand Bombardier, his brothers Alphonse-Raymond, Léopold and Gérard, and Secretary-Treasurer Marie-Jeanne Dupaul were the only shareholders. Shortly thereafter, Joseph-Armand's oldest son, Germain, and an engineer named Roland Saint-Pierre also became shareholders. This team would be responsible for the growth of L'Auto-Neige Bombardier over the next 22 years.

The 1942 management team: (top) Alphonse-Raymond Bombardier, Vice-President; Joseph-Armand Bombardier, President; and Marie-Jeanne Dupaul, Secretary-Treasurer; (bottom) Gérard Bombardier, Production Manager; and Léopold Bombardier, Maintenance Manager.

*A 1939 advertising flyer which was mailed
to a wide range of potential clients.*

Various versions of this 1941 B12 snowmobile were produced up until 1982.

Wartime production

While World War II was putting civilian snowmobile production on hold at the brand-new Valcourt factory, the Canadian military and its allies were on the lookout for vehicles that could transport troops over snowbound battlefields.

In response to a service tender by Joseph-Armand Bombardier, the Canadian Ministry of Supplies and Munitions bought a B12 for testing in 1941.

Early the following year, Joseph-Armand Bombardier was given the go-ahead to build a military snowmobile prototype based on the B12. The new machine was to be used to move troops in an operation in the north of Norway.

Within weeks the inventor designed and built the prototype, which would later be called the B1*. The new snowmobile featured several technical innovations which he would patent both in Canada and the United States. The Canadian army placed an order for 130 of the vehicles.

The four-month delivery deadline was considered beyond the capacity of the Valcourt factory. Therefore, most of the production had to take place in Montréal factories, under Joseph-Armand Bombardier's supervision.

In 1943, the armed forces called upon the inventor once again, this time for the design of an armoured all-track snowmobile – the Kaki* –

which was ready for testing by the spring of the very same year.

The encouraging test results of the Kaki led the inventor to develop the Mark* I, which was the first of a series of armoured snowmobiles. It was greeted with enthusiasm by the military but, once again, most of the manufacturing was handled by other factories. Until the end of the war, and as late as in 1946, the army made various changes to the vehicle; it became the Mark 2, also known as the Penguin, and then the Mark 3.

More than 1,900 tracked vehicles based on Joseph-Armand Bombardier's designs were built for military applications between 1942 and 1946. Unfortunately, except for surviving on the construction of prototypes and some parts, the Valcourt factory saw little profit from the military snowmobiles.

The inventor also had to give up the royalties for the use of his patents in military vehicles. However, his participation in the war effort did enable him to hone his technical expertise and to improve the various systems of his vehicles. The postwar Bombardier vehicles thus benefited from four major improvements that were patented between 1943 and 1946: the Wheel Mounting, the Traction Device, the Vehicle Spring Suspension and the Rubberized Sprocket Wheel.

*The Sprocket Wheel, developed in 1943
and patented in 1945, was
a major improvement over the 1936 model.*

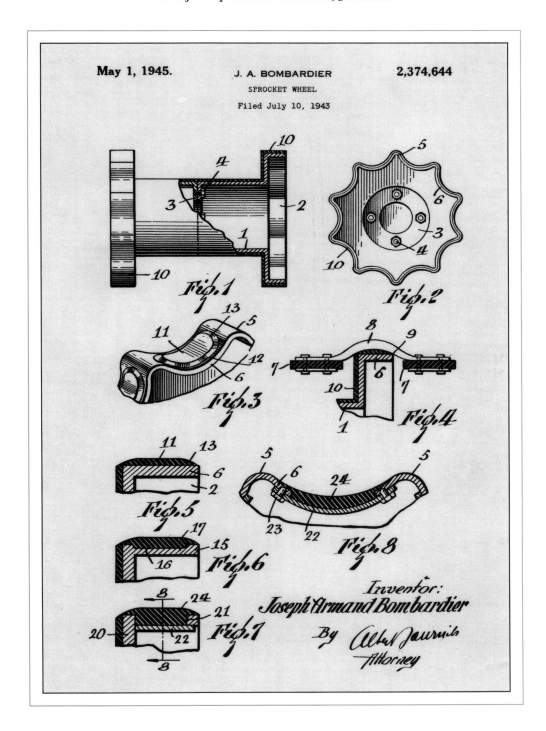

May 1, 1945.

J. A. BOMBARDIER

2,374,644

SPROCKET WHEEL

Filed July 10, 1943

Inventor:
Joseph Armand Bombardier

By Albert Jaurich
Attorney

The trials of the Kaki armoured snowmobile took place in the Valcourt region in 1943.

In February 1946, during a Canadian Army operation,
12 Penguin snowmobiles travelled over a 1,600-kilometre route between
Churchill, Manitoba, the Arctic Circle and Edmonton, Alberta.

Postwar prosperity

Despite the restrictions, civilian snowmobile production at Valcourt continued during the war in response to the needs of special permit holders. In fact, production increased from year to year, going from 27 units in 1942-43 to 230 in 1945-46.

With the gradual lifting of wartime restrictions, demand for snow vehicles increased considerably, until the 1940 factory could no longer cope. Following an initial expansion in 1946, L'Auto-Neige Bombardier opened a vast assembly facility in 1947, with a yearly production capacity of 1,000 units.

Two products ensured the Company's prosperity throughout the postwar years: the B12 and the C18*.

The multi-purpose B12 was used for public transport, freight transport, mail delivery, and ambulance and rescue services. Public utilities used it to reach their lines, and prospectors and forest operators used it to reach remote sites. Between 1945 and 1952, L'Auto-Neige Bombardier sold some 1,600 B12 vehicles.

The Valcourt company began building a new "school" snowmobile in 1945 to meet the winter transportation needs of Protestant schools in Québec's Eastern Townships. A larger version of the B12, the C18, could carry up to 25 schoolchildren. Over the following years it would become immensely popular throughout Québec and Ontario.

Beyond the quality and usefulness of the Bombardier vehicles, good promotion and a well-organized sales network accounted for the commercial success of L'Auto-Neige Bombardier. Under Alphonse-Raymond Bombardier's energetic management, the sales and distribution network spread across Canada and to the major centres of the northern United States. Breakthroughs were also made in other countries, in response to specific needs.

Now that the commercial operations were well established, the inventor was able to return to research, concentrating on improvements to make the 1937 track stronger and more flexible.

In 1947-48, L'Auto-Neige Bombardier's sales volume reached $2.3 million, compared with $211,800 in 1942-43. A profit of $324,000 was proof positive of the renewed prosperity.

In 1948-49,[1] however, the Québec government implemented a new snow-removal policy for rural roads that would leave the snowmobile industry hard-hit. Orders at L'Auto-Neige Bombardier were on the decline, and within a year sales dropped by $1 million.

Once again, Joseph-Armand Bombardier had to refocus his company's mission.

(1) On December 16, 1949, the name of the Corporation was amended by letters patent to: L'Auto-Neige Bombardier Limitée / Bombardier Snowmobile Limited.

*After the war, the many applications of the B12 became apparent,
including postal services and log transportation.*

Many of the licensed L'Auto-Neige Bombardier representatives
were automobile dealerships, which had the necessary repair shops and
spare part stores to ensure good after-sales service.

Protestant school boards in Québec's Eastern Townships became
the first owners of the C18 snowmobile in November 1945.

New products, new markets

During the winter of 1948-49, Joseph-Armand Bombardier began intensive research to create new products that would supplement the snowmobile.

At the research centre he had recently built in Kingsbury, near Valcourt, he modified the B12 to make it suitable for loading and transporting lumber, as well as for other customer needs. He also developed several prototypes, including the all-track C4* and the B5*, which had interchangeable skis and wheels.

But in the opinion of the inventor, none of these vehicles would trigger the demand needed to return to previous activity levels.

The Company's recovery began in the fall of 1949 with the sale of a traction mechanism perfected by Joseph-Armand Bombardier and based on an idea developed by his brother Gérard. Designed to improve the performance of tractors in muddy terrain, the Tractor Tracking Attachment (TTA) was an instant success in the agricultural sector and with American tractor manufacturers. Between 1949 and 1954, this device would sell by the thousands across North America and in areas of Europe and South America.

During this period, the inventor continued his research in the hope of developing all-terrain tracked vehicles for the mining, oil and forestry industries.

In 1953, the search for new products was bolstered by the invention of an unbreakable and warp-proof all-rubber sprocket, and the design of a new vulcanizing machine that allowed the production of seamless and shock-resistant tracks.

That same year, and with the help of his father, Germain Bombardier, Joseph-Armand's oldest son, created L'Auto-Neige Bombardier's first subsidiary, Rockland Accessories Ltd. Located in Kingsbury, the new company built all the rubber parts used in the Bombardier vehicles.

The Muskeg* ("swamp" in Amerindian) tractor was one of the first vehicles to benefit from the 1953 innovations. Rolled off the Valcourt assembly line in 1953, the Muskeg was very successful because it performed multiple transportation and operation functions in difficult terrain. Modern versions of the Muskeg are still being sold throughout the world today.

Another impressive success from this fertile period was the development of the J5* tractor in 1955. The J5 was the first tracked vehicle specifically designed for forestry. Equipped with a shovel, this vehicle later gave birth to the smaller SW* tractor, still in use today for urban snow removal.

Through 1958, 1959 and 1960, Joseph-Armand Bombardier developed several vehicles for forestry operations and oil exploration. But a change was in the offing, and it would have a profound effect on the Valcourt company's orientation.

The TTA was designed by Gérard Bombardier in 1949 to improve tractor traction. It included an extra wheel with independent suspension and a track for each side of the tractor.

Faced with a lack of flexibility on the part of his rubber parts suppliers, high prices and poor quality, Joseph-Armand Bombardier invented a circular vulcanizing machine in 1953.

Joseph-Armand Bombardier considered the Muskeg one of his greatest successes.
It was launched in 1953.

The Muskeg was used to transport material during a 1957
Antarctic expedition led by Sir Vivian Fuchs.

*The J5 tractor underwent some of its testing at sites owned by
the Quebec North Shore forestry company during the winter of 1954-55.*

The VFB logging machine, also called the "steel lumberjack,"
used for tree cutting in 1961.

The birth of a new industry

The 1959-1973 period began with an event which would exert a huge influence on the future of the Valcourt company: the invention of the Ski-Doo snowmobile.

By the end of the 1950s, L'Auto-Neige Bombardier had returned to prosperity, and continued growth was ensured by the diversification of its products and markets. In 1958-59, sales reached $3.5 million, while profits stood at around $825,000.

In 1957, while still managing the business, Joseph-Armand Bombardier stepped up his research on the small snowmobile he had dreamed of since childhood. The use of an all-rubber track reinforced with hidden metal rods and the arrival of lighter engines made his dream come true at last.

Designed and patented by Germain Bombardier, Joseph-Armand's oldest son, the new track was superior to any other comparable product then available. What made it stand out was not only its lightness and flexibility, but also its traction power.

After evaluating the performance of various engines and designing several chassis and body shapes, Joseph-Armand Bombardier settled on a Kohler four-stroke engine and perfected a light vehicle that met his own approval. During the fall of 1958, he and his team worked intensely on a prototype.

The first field tests were conducted in the Valcourt area during the winter of 1958-59. The trials wound up in Northern Ontario, where Father Maurice Ouimet, a Valcourt native and close friend of Joseph-Armand Bombardier, ran a Catholic mission for Ojibway Indians. The results were conclusive: the vehicle met its inventor's expectations.

Mass production began during the fall of 1959, and 225 Ski-Doo snowmobiles were sold the following winter for about $900 each. The Ski-Doo snowmobile had just come into being, and along with it, a whole new industry.

Led from the outset by L'Auto-Neige Bombardier, this industry was to see its heyday in the late 1960s and early 1970s.

*Prototypes of light vehicles which were the forerunners of
the Ski-Doo snowmobile. Joseph-Armand Bombardier tested them
himself over the winters of 1957 and 1958.*

*The 1959-60 model was equipped with 1.5-metre-long (five-foot) wooden skis
and a coil-spring suspension system. It was the first of
its kind to make use of an all-rubber track, and its centrifugal clutch
consisted of only six moving parts. Driven by a Kohler four-stroke engine,
the vehicle could reach a top speed of 40 kilometres per hour (25 mph).*

The first successes

The new machine, which Joseph-Armand Bombardier patented in Canada in 1960 and in the United States in 1962, was unique: it brought a practical, safe and economical solution to the problems of individual transportation over snow in isolated regions. It quickly found a clientele among missionaries, trappers, prospectors, surveyors, game wardens, government agencies and other people who had to get around in snowbound regions.

But the snowmobiling craze was what triggered the product's huge popularity and, by the same token, the growth of L'Auto-Neige Bombardier.

The advertisements for the first commercial model already emphasized its sporting aspect: "Outdoor enthusiasts looking for new thrills in winter sports will find them with the Bombardier Ski-Doo..."

Demand was slow to take off, but picked up with each new year as the promotion and sales network developed. From an output of 225 units in 1959-60, production rose to 250 for the 1960-61 models, 1,200 for 1961-62, 2,502 for 1962-63 and then to 8,210 for 1963-64. The rapid growth of production brought on successive waves of reorganization and expansion at the Valcourt facilities.

Technically, the 1959-60 model saw only minor changes over the next two seasons, but substantial modifications were incorporated into the 1962-63 Ski-Doo snowmobile. A fibreglass cab was added, giving it more fluid lines, and after an exhaustive evaluation of all engines then available, Joseph-Armand Bombardier replaced the Kohler and JLO ones with the renowned Austrian Rotax engine.

The use of fibreglass for the Ski-Doo cab prompted Joseph-Armand Bombardier to create a new company. Specializing in fibreglass parts, Roski Ltd. was formed in 1963 in Roxton Falls, near Valcourt.

Between 1960 and 1964, snowmobiling spread first across Québec, then to Ontario and New England, and then to other areas of North America and parts of Europe. The sport became organized around the activities of clubs which attracted a steady stream of new members.

Though his invention gave birth to this new sport, Joseph-Armand Bombardier would only live to see the first signs of the snowmobile's phenomenal success. His death on February 18, 1964, marked the end of a rich and full life. The helm of L'Auto-Neige Bombardier passed to the next generation.

The 1960-61 Ski-Doo model. In its second year on the market,
the bright yellow Ski-Doo machine became a familiar sight throughout
the North American winter landscape.

While responding to growing demand from sport enthusiasts,
the Valcourt company did not forget the vehicle's original utilitarian purposes.

One of the first snowmobile races was held in 1962 on the Rivière des Prairies,
in front of the Commodore Yacht Club near Montréal.

A prolific inventor, Joseph-Armand Bombardier
obtained over 40 patents in less than 25 years. A wise entrepreneur,
he laid the foundation of what would become
one of Canada's biggest manufacturing companies.

A legacy for the future

Upon his death at age 56, Joseph-Armand Bombardier left behind a healthy and financially sound company.

From $3.5 million in 1958-59, L'Auto-Neige Bombardier's sales climbed to $10 million in 1963-64, and profits grew from $825,000 to $2 million. The manufacture and sale of industrial vehicles, particularly the Muskeg and J5 tractors, ensured a solid revenue base, while the Ski-Doo snowmobile offered excellent growth potential.

The Company's succession had been carefully prepared. Les Entreprises de J. Armand Bombardier Ltée, a family holding, had been founded in 1954 with the inventor's five children as shareholders. By the summer of 1963, it had gained full control of L'Auto-Neige Bombardier when the minority shareholders' stakes were bought back. In addition, the founder had left specific instructions as to the management structure which he thought would be best for the Company.

In 1964, Joseph-Armand Bombardier's oldest son Germain, who had been Vice-President of L'Auto-Neige Bombardier since 1956, was named President. He held this position for two years, after which he retired for health reasons.

Laurent Beaudoin, Joseph-Armand Bombardier's son-in-law, took over the presidency in 1966. He had joined the Company in 1963 as Controller and had been appointed General Manager after the death of his father-in-law. Supporting him in his new role was the Board of directors, of which he was a member, as were three other family members – J.R. André Bombardier, Gaston Bissonnette and Jean-Louis Fontaine, and two consultants specialized in finance and law – Jean Paul Gagnon, from the chartered accountant firm Bélanger, Dallaire, Gagnon & Associés, of Quebec City, and Charles Leblanc, from the law firm Leblanc Delorme et Associés, of Sherbrooke.

The new president could also count on a dynamic management team which was ready for the rapid growth of the late 1960s. Under his leadership, L'Auto-Neige Bombardier would take full advantage of the strong demand for snowmobiles, despite a proliferation of new manufacturers vying for the growing market.

The name L'Auto-Neige Bombardier was changed on February 24, 1967. From then on, the Company would operate under the name of Bombardier Limitée.

Germain Bombardier, who worked for his father for 15 years,
became President of L'Auto-Neige Bombardier in 1964.
A gifted mechanic, he already had several patents to his name and had
managed the Rockland Accessories subsidiary since 1953.

42

Laurent Beaudoin was only 27 years old when he became
President and General Manager of L'Auto-Neige Bombardier in 1966.

The golden age
of the snowmobile

From the mid-sixties onward, the North American snowmobile industry took on a frenzied pace. From an estimated 60,000 units sold in 1965-66, retail sales peaked at 495,000 units in 1971-72, at which time over 100 manufacturers were competing in the market.

With 90% of its activity tied to snowmobiles, Bombardier saw equally impressive growth. Its revenues and profits rose from $20 million and $3 million respectively in 1965-66 to $183 million and $12 million in 1971-72.

In 1966, the new management team set out to take the North American market by storm. Averaging 30 years of age, they developed an aggressive marketing strategy focusing on the snowmobile as a sport and leisure activity.

The different models, previously identified by letters, now sported new, evocative names: Alpine*, Chalet*, Olympic*, Nordic*, Skandic*, T'NT*, Élan* and Blizzard*.

Sophisticated brochures highlighting the pleasures of the great outdoors were printed each year and the same themes were used for mass-media advertising campaigns. The advertising budget alone rose from $32,000 in 1963-64 to $5 million in 1969.

Aside from direct promotion, Bombardier also took advantage of every opportunity to spread the word about its product. For example, in 1967 and 1968, the Company financed two expeditions – on Ski-Doo snowmobiles – to the North Pole, headed by Ralph Plaisted. On April 19, 1968, the success of the second attempt amply demonstrated the product's reliability, endurance and strength.

The Company also helped establish several regional races, along with the World Snowmobile Championship held annually at Eagle River, Wisconsin. While these competitions put the snowmobile in the limelight, they were also an invaluable source of technical information for new models and for continuous performance improvement.

In addition, Bombardier encouraged a more rational approach to snowmobiling by helping to develop groomed trails and establish safety regulations.

The solid planning and organization that went into the distribution and sales network were important assets for the implementation of the commercial strategy. Backed by strong technical and promotional support, the Bombardier dealerships were given an additional boost with the creation of two subsidiaries providing inventory financing services: Crédit Bombardier Limitée in Valcourt, Québec, and Bombardier Credit, Inc. (now called Bombardier Capital Inc.) in Burlington, Vermont.

In fact, the strength of the sales network was one of the main factors behind the continued leadership of the Ski-Doo brand in the increasingly competitive snowmobile market. At the Valcourt facility, this meant an increase in annual output from some 23,000 units in 1965-66 to 115,000 in 1968-69 and 210,000 in 1971-72.

The Ski-Doo Olympic model played a crucial role in the Plaisted expedition of 1968.
A nephew of the inventor, Jean-Luc Bombardier (below right),
took part in the 1,330-kilometre (825-mile) journey to the North Pole.

At a 1971 Ski-Doo distributor meeting in Rovaniemi, Finland,
Bombardier President and Chief Executive Officer Laurent Beaudoin
was proclaimed Honorary Laplander by "King" Allalarouka.

Launched in 1970, the Skidozer* groomer was central to
Operation Snoplan, which was initiated in 1971 to promote the development
and maintenance of groomed snowmobile trails.

As snowmobiling became better organized, groomed trails
spread across the snowy regions of North America.

A business in its prime

In 1969, with the snowmobile becoming a much sought-after consumer good, Bombardier's future growth seemed assured. The decision was made to go public and became official through letters patent dated January 23, 1969. This resulted in a public offering of two million shares by Les Entreprises de J. Armand Bombardier, and in Bombardier stock being listed on the Montréal and Toronto stock exchanges.

In addition to enabling investors to participate in the Company's progress, the creation of a market for Bombardier shares provided a practical source of financing for further vertical integration.

Already under way when the shares were issued, this vertical integration was intended to ensure the reliability and quality of supply. Since 1957 the Company had owned Les Industries Rockland Ltée,[1] which produced tracks and other rubber parts for Bombardier's recreational and industrial vehicles. In 1968 the Company had acquired Les Plastiques LaSalle Inc., a plastic parts manufacturer, and in early 1969 it had taken control of 50% of Ville-Marie Rembourrage Ltée, a company specializing in foam-rubber seats. Also in early 1969, Roski Ltée,[2] a manufacturer of fibreglass parts, became a wholly owned subsidiary of Bombardier Limitée.

Afterwards, Bombardier added Jarry Précision Ltée, a precision metal tool and parts manufacturer, and Placage Automatique Drummond Inc., a chrome-plating company, to its acquisitions list. The Company also took over the remaining 50% of Ville-Marie Rembourrage Ltée.

In 1970, Bombardier completed the biggest of this series of acquisitions by buying the Austrian firm Lohnerwerke GmbH and its affiliate Rotax-Werk AG. The two were subsequently merged with Bombardier under the name Bombardier-Rotax GmbH.

Founded in 1823, Lohnerwerke was dedicated mainly to manufacturing tramways at its Vienna factory – and its many years of experience would prove very helpful to Bombardier's diversification into rail transit equipment a few years later. But in 1970, Bombardier was more interested in the operations of Rotax-Werk, based in Gunskirchen. In fact, Rotax-Werk had been the supplier of the two-stroke Rotax engine for the Ski-Doo snowmobiles since 1962. This acquisition gave Bombardier technological control over the snowmobile's core component, while reinforcing the Company's manufacturing structure as well as its research and development capabilities.

In 1971, Bombardier acquired a competitor, Les Industries Bouchard Inc., which operated a plant at La Pocatière, Québec. At the time, Bouchard's Moto-Ski* snowmobile was the third best seller on the market, and the acquisition consolidated Bombardier's market share.

But as early as the following year, the market began showing signs of a decline which would radically transform the industry.

(1) Founded by Germain Bombardier in 1953 under the name of Rockland Accessories Ltd.

(2) Founded by Joseph-Armand Bombardier in 1963, and a subsidiary of Les Entreprises de J. Armand Bombardier until 1969.

*The Bombardier Limitée Board of Directors in 1969: (front centre)
Laurent Beaudoin, President and General Manager; (back centre)
Jean Paul Gagnon, Vice-President, Finance; (left to right) Gaston Bissonnette,
Vice-President, Research and Development, Recreational Products Division;
Charles Leblanc, Executive Vice-President and Secretary; J.R. André Bombardier,
Vice-President, Industrial Products Division; John N. Cole, Director;
and Jean-Louis Fontaine, Vice-President, Production, Recreational Products Division.*

A snowmobile assembly line at the Valcourt plant.
Once vertical integration was completed in 1972,
over 85% of the content of Bombardier snowmobiles
was built by the Company and its subsidiaries.

*Following the acquisition of Rotax-Werk, Bombardier proceeded to expand
the Gunskirchen plant. President and General Manager
Laurent Beaudoin (centre) examines the model for the new section,
along with Rotax General Manager Helmut Rothe (left)
and Rotax Assistant General Manager Karl Pötzlberger (right).*

52

*Horizontal integration, which proceeded on a somewhat more modest scale
than did the vertical integration program, saw the acquisition of two companies
specializing in the manufacture and sale of clothing and accessories:
Walker Manufacturing Company Ltd. and Ski-Doo Sports Ltée, respectively.*

The acquisition of the Moto-Ski brand
enabled Bombardier to expand its dealership network.

The first years of diversification

The second half of the 1970s was a crucial period in the evolution of Bombardier, as the Company started on a path of diversification which would place it among the leaders of Canadian industry in less than 15 years.

The first energy crisis, in the fall of 1973, dealt a hard blow to the snowmobile market, where growth had already slowed noticeably in the previous two years due to saturation of demand. North American retail sales, which had peaked at 495,000 units in 1971-72, went into free fall during the following seasons, reaching about 315,000 units in 1974-75. The industry collapsed: out of 100 manufacturers in 1971, only six were able to stay in business.

Bombardier, one of the survivors, was determined to remain in the marketplace, keep its leading position, and take advantage of the recovery which would come sooner or later.

To achieve a better balance in the Company's activities, management focused efforts on finding new products and new markets. One of the most important projects undertaken during this period was the 1972 launch of the Can-Am* off-road motorcycle. Like the snowmobile, this product used the Rotax engine. Many of its parts were supplied by the Bombardier subsidiaries, while distribution was handled through the existing dealer network.

The subsidiaries were for their part encouraged to expand their activities. One of them, Roski Ltd., was entrusted with the manufacturing of the "Invitation" fibreglass sailboat, which Bombardier introduced to the marketplace in the spring of 1974. Roski also produced the seats for the stadium and velodrome that were being built for the 1976 Montréal Olympic Games.

In February 1973 Bombardier acquired a 60% interest in Héroux Limited. Héroux's plants, located in the Montréal area at Longueuil and Saint-Jean, were specialized in the manufacture and maintenance of landing gear for civil and military aircraft.

These various measures were not sufficient, however, to ensure the desired balance. Bombardier began a diversification strategy based on two criteria: existing skills in production management, and manufacturing specialties that were counter-cyclical and compatible with the existing facilities.

An opportunity which fit these criteria appeared in 1974 in the field of rail transit. It would enable the Company to lay the foundation for medium-term growth.

President and Chief Executive Officer Laurent Beaudoin and
Mrs. Yvonne Bombardier, widow of Joseph-Armand Bombardier, attended the celebration
that marked the production of the one millionth Ski-Doo snowmobile in 1973.

*In motocross competitions, Bombardier's Can-Am motorcycles took
the top three places in the 1974 American Championship, 250cc category, and a
gold medal at the International Championships held in Italy.*

In 1974, Bombardier added the Invitation sailboat
to its line of recreational products. The first model was followed
by two others: the Bombardier 3.8 and Bombardier 4.8.

The Montréal subway

While it precipitated a decline in the snow-mobile market, the 1973 oil crisis also led to a recovery in the mass transit sector.

When the City of Montréal announced an expansion program for its subway system in early 1974, Bombardier decided to become a rolling stock manufacturer. For the Company, the project presented an opportunity to enter a sector that held good prospects and met its diversification criteria. The Company also saw the project as a way to retain its qualified workforce, and to give a new mission to the Moto-Ski snowmobile plant at La Pocatière, Québec.

During the construction of the Montréal subway in 1963, the original rolling stock had been supplied by the Vickers company under licence from the French manufacturer CIMT-Lorraine (later absorbed by the Alsthom group). As the Vickers licence had expired, Bombardier acquired it in order to make a bid to Montréal.

A team was put together to prepare the tender with technical backup from CIMT. The team worked under the management of Jean-Louis Fontaine, then Vice-President of the Company, who would later lead the engineering group on this project.

In May 1974, Montréal's transit authority, the Montreal Urban Community Transit Commission (MUCTC),[1] awarded Bombardier an order worth $117.8 million for 423 subway cars, to be produced over a four-year period.

The responsibility for carrying out this order was assigned to Raymond Royer, who joined Bombardier in 1974 as General Manager of the subsidiary Bombardier Transportation Products Ltd.

The bulk of the manufacturing and assembly work was done at the La Pocatière plant, which was modified, enlarged, and retooled. A part of the Valcourt facilities was also modified to produce the subway cars' bogies.

In barely two years, Bombardier put together the project team, completed the technology transfer, reorganized the plants and began production. The first cars were delivered in July 1976.

The order, which was completed in 1978, allowed Bombardier to establish itself firmly in a new field of activity. Building on this initial contract, over the next few years the Company set out to conquer the North American rail transit equipment market which, at the time, offered excellent growth prospects.

When Bombardier entered this new field, snowmobiles still represented 90% of its business. A new corporate team was formed to manage and promote the diversification.

(1) This designation would later be changed to the Société de transport de la Communauté urbaine de Montréal (STCUM).

*In 1976, Raymond Royer (left), General Manager of the subsidiary Bombardier
Transportation Products Ltd., with Mr. Jean-Guy Massé, Assistant Superintendent of the BTM
(Montréal's transit authority), in front of the first rail transit car ever delivered by
the Company. Raymond Royer became Executive Vice-President of Bombardier in 1984,
and President and Chief Operating Officer in 1986.*

Production of Montréal subway cars at the La Pocatière plant,
which is the most modern of its kind in North America.

The rubber-tired subway car technology used in Montréal is also found
in Paris, Mexico City, Caracas and Santiago (Chile).
Some of Bombardier's subsidiaries worked on the Montréal order.

Expansion in transportation equipment

As the next step in the Company's diversification into railway equipment, management decided to integrate Bombardier's activities with those of MLW-Worthington Limitée (MLW), a locomotive and diesel engine manufacturer that had been founded in Montréal in 1902.

The industrial complex thus formed in 1976 operated under the corporate name of Bombardier-MLW Ltée, which was changed to Bombardier Inc. in 1981.

At this stage, Bombardier's priority was to widen its range of rail transit equipment. MLW's technology included the LRC (Light, Rapid, Comfortable) train designed to run at high speed on conventional North American track.

Supported by the experience gained in the Montréal subway contract and determined to avoid the difficulties which had caused most of the great U.S. rolling stock manufacturers to abandon the field in the 1960s, Bombardier chose to acquire proven technologies, master them, and adapt them to the needs of the marketplace.

The application of this strategy soon led to the signing of two licence agreements: one in 1979 with Belgian manufacturer BN Constructions Ferroviaires et Métalliques S.A. for light rail vehicles; the other in 1980 with Pullman Incorporated, of the United States, for the Erie-Lackawanna* push-pull commuter cars.

In terms of sales, several "firsts" were achieved by Bombardier between 1977 and 1981: its first U.S. transit equipment order in 1977, for 36 bi-level self-propelled commuter cars for the Chicago South Suburban Mass Transit District; its first sale of LRC trains to VIA Rail Canada in 1978 (21 locomotives and 50 cars); and its first major breakthrough in the United States in 1980, with a New Jersey Transit Corporation (NJ Transit) order for 117 Erie-Lackawanna commuter cars.

The list of firsts continued to grow in 1981, when Bombardier landed an order for 180 subway cars for Mexico City. That same year, the sale of 26 light rail vehicles to the Tri-County Metropolitan Transportation District, of Portland, Oregon, represented Bombardier's first success in an international call for tenders.

The diversification into mass transit was not accomplished without difficulty, however. The "Buy America Act" of 1978 presented an obstacle to Bombardier's penetration of the American market. The Act notably required that 50% of the content of vehicles destined for the American market should be made in the U.S., and that final assembly be performed on American soil. In order both to conform to this law and to establish a stronger presence in its main market, in 1980 the Company decided to build a final assembly plant in Barre, Vermont.

That year would also witness Bombardier's entry into another field of activity.

*The manufacturing work on the LRC trains ordered by Via Rail Canada was
shared between the Montréal plant (Rail Products Division), which built the locomotives,
and the La Pocatière plant (Mass Transit Division), which built the cars.*

*The 1981 order for the Mexico City subway cars was,
at the time, the largest export order to be won by a Canadian or
American mass transit equipment manufacturer.*

*The Barre, Vermont plant, completed in 1981, was first used for
the final assembly of the New Jersey cars, and subsequently for the final assembly of
all rail transit vehicles destined for the American market.*

A new field of activity

In its continuing quest for diversification, at the beginning of the 1980s Bombardier decided to enter the military equipment field, having learned that the Department of National Defence was planning to invite proposals for the supply of trucks to renew the Canadian Forces fleet which was over 25 years old.

Adopting the same strategy that had succeeded in rail transit equipment, the Company decided to base its bid for a foothold in this new market on proven technology. Bombardier in fact held the Canadian manufacturing and marketing rights to a 2½-ton truck, as well as the right to sell the truck in certain other countries under a 1977 agreement with AM General Corporation (AMG), of the U.S.

The right moment arrived at the end of 1979, when the Department issued its call for tenders. The Company's offer, based on the AMG truck, was presented in May 1980 by the newly created Logistics Equipment Division. In March 1981, the Canadian government awarded Bombardier an order for 2,767 units.

Thirteen months later, the first truck rolled out of the modern plant that had been set up at the Valcourt facilities for military vehicle production. Deliveries were completed in 1983 and were ahead of schedule.

Shortly after obtaining this first order, Bombardier was led to expand its range of logistics vehicles by the prospect of another market at National Defence. Through an agreement signed in March 1982 with Volkswagen AG of Germany, the Company obtained the design and manufacturing technology for a light military truck known as Iltis*.

Bombardier was awarded a contract to supply 1,900 Iltis trucks to the Canadian Forces in the fall of 1983. This contract not only consolidated the Company's position as a manufacturer of logistics equipment, but also laid a solid foundation for the development of export markets.

A major breakthrough occurred in the European market in January 1985, when an agreement to supply 2,500 Iltis trucks to the Belgian army was concluded.

Before committing itself to the manufacture and supply of military trucks, Bombardier had sought and received informal recognition from Canadian authorities as a Centre of Excellence for this type of equipment. Indeed, before fully developing its capacity in this specialized niche, the Company had to be assured of a base in its home market. As a result of subsequent changes in government policies, however, Bombardier had no choice but to abandon the logistics vehicle market in 1989. Nevertheless, it would continue to supply spare parts for the vehicles it had already delivered.

*Dubbed "the army's workhorse," Bombardier's modified AMG truck
was the first Canadian-built 2½-ton military truck.*

*In all, Bombardier supplied 2,500 Iltis vehicles to the Canadian Forces,
2,500 to the Belgian army and 600 to the German army.*

Major markets
and explosive growth

Without a doubt, the years between 1982 and 1988 represent the most impressive period of expansion in Bombardier's history.

In 1982, business volume reached the half-billion-dollar mark. That same year, Bombardier defined its mission statement to read: "The Company must endeavour to assert its leadership in Canada, and to take its place as one of the foremost producers of transportation equipment and related products in the world." Decisions, action and success would soon flow from this mission statement.

Bombardier pursued its penetration of the North American market for rail transit equipment and saw its leadership confirmed by the award of a major contract to build cars for the New York City subway system in 1982. The Company also laid the foundation of its European industrial expansion in this field by acquiring a 45% interest in the Belgian manufacturer BN Constructions Ferroviaires et Métalliques s.a. in 1986.

In an effort to rationalize recreational vehicle operations, in early 1983 the manufacturing subsidiaries were sold to Camoplast Inc., a company created by a group of management employees. On the other hand, Bombardier gained ownership of the diesel engine technology which powered its locomotives with the 1984 acquisition of Alco Power Inc., of Auburn, New York.

A year later, another subsidiary, Héroux Inc., was sold to two of its directors, since its activities were not at the time compatible with Bombardier's general orientation and long-term goals.

With reasonable growth ensured by its ongoing business, Bombardier remained on the lookout for new diversification opportunities. Thus, in 1986 the Company launched into the field of aerospace by acquiring Canadair. Bombardier's business volume immediately jumped to over $1 billion.

In only four years, Bombardier had doubled its size to join the ranks of Canada's 20 largest manufacturing companies.

*The Ski-Doo snowmobile, which celebrated its 25th anniversary in 1983-84,
had seen impressive technological progress since its introduction.*

*Light rail vehicles, or articulated tramways, were delivered to
Portland, Oregon, in 1984 and 1985. They were based on BN technology,
to which Bombardier held the rights through a licensing agreement.*

Following Bombardier's move into aerospace, operations management was split into two major groups in 1987: the Transportation Equipment Group and the Aerospace Group, led by President Raymond Royer (centre) and President Donald C. Lowe (right), respectively. Both reported to Chairman and Chief Executive Officer Laurent Beaudoin (left).

The New York contract, a decisive breakthrough

To strengthen its position in the North American transit equipment industry, Bombardier decided in 1981 to concentrate on a major new market that was emerging in New York City. The Metropolitan Transportation Authority (MTA) of New York had announced that it would purchase over 1,500 steel-wheeled subway cars, to renew its fleet of rolling stock.

A first order for 325 cars had gone to Kawasaki Heavy Industries Ltd., and Bombardier perceived the advantage of offering compatible equipment. To that end, negotiations were begun with the Japanese manufacturer to build cars under licence.

In December 1981, the MTA called for tenders for 825 additional steel-wheeled subway cars. Three companies including Bombardier submitted bids.

Intense negotiations followed the February 1982 tendering of bids. All of the technical, financial and legal resources of the Mass Transit Division and corporate office were put behind Bombardier's New York negotiating team.

On June 10, 1982, an agreement was reached between the MTA and Bombardier. This was the first step toward what would be known as "the mass transit equipment deal of the century" and "the biggest export contract ever awarded to a Canadian manufacturer." Upon completion in 1987, the transaction had a value of over $1 billion (Canadian).

The first car rolled off the assembly line in 1984, and it was subjected to a battery of exhaustive tests at the La Pocatière facility, which had been equipped with a new test track. Later that year, the Mass Transit Division delivered the first 10-car train to the MTA for further testing. For this round of testing, the cars had to run continuously for 30 days without a single failure. After an intensive break-in period, the testing stage was successfully completed in April 1985, and the active manufacturing phase began.

At the height of production, the pace reached two cars a day, and employment on the contract rose to over 2,000 workers. The contract was completed in September 1987, one month ahead of schedule. It had established Bombardier as the leading North American manufacturer of rail transit equipment.

In 1987, the La Pocatière and Barre facilities experienced an exceptional level of activity. Even as they built the remaining 294 New York subway cars, they were also building 136 commuter rail cars for various other American transit authorities, including the Metro-North Commuter Railroad serving New York City's northern suburbs.

That same year, Bombardier undertook its first fully integrated project in transportation equipment. The project called for the supply of seven General Motors locomotives and 35 commuter train cars to the Southeastern Pennsylvania Transportation Authority, as well as the construction and operation of a maintenance facility in the Philadelphia area, and the development of an innovative financing package.

The final signing of the New York subway car contract on November 15, 1982:
(left to right) Raymond Royer, President and Chief Operating Officer of Bombardier;
Laurent Beaudoin, Chairman and Chief Executive Officer of Bombardier;
Richard Ravitch, then Chairman of the MTA; The Honourable Gerald A. Regan,
then Canadian Minister of State for International Trade; and
The Honourable Edward Lumley, then Canadian Minister of Industry
and Regional Economic Expansion.

Since they were put into service, the 825 cars Bombardier delivered to New York have had the highest performance rating of any in the MTA fleet.

Based on a Pullman design, the Erie-Lackawanna commuter train car is
one of Bombardier's most successful transit vehicles. Between 1981
and 1992, the La Pocatière and Barre plants produced over 745 of these cars.

Commuter train cars under repair at the Bombardier-built
service centre in the Philadelphia area.

A North American leader, master of its technology

When the construction of the New York subway cars began, Bombardier had the capacity to provide the North American market with steel-wheeled and rubber-tired subway cars, light rail vehicles (also called tramways), self-propelled commuter cars, commuter coaches and LRC mainline trains. This product line, the most extensive offered in North America, met the needs of urban, commuter and inter-city rail transit.

With a vision of the evolution of the North American market, in 1984 Bombardier acquired technologies which opened up new markets for turnkey systems and transcontinental passenger transportation.

First came an agreement with the Walt Disney Company for the exclusive rights to market, build and operate the WEDway PeopleMover (automatic shuttles) and Monorail systems originally developed by the Disney organization. To make the most of the potential for integrated transportation systems, Bombardier created an American subsidiary called The Transportation Group Inc. (TGI) in 1985, giving it a mandate to market these products in the United States. Early in 1987, following an international call for tenders, the subsidiary won a contract to supply 72 monorail cars for the Walt Disney World amusement park in Florida.

Second was a licence agreement signed with Pullman for the "Horizon" single-level transit railcar. An initial order for this equipment was awarded by the National Railroad Passenger Corporation (Amtrak) in 1988.

A management decision to go beyond simple licence agreements led to the December 1986 acquisition of Pullman Technology Inc., of Chicago, the company that owned the design technology for all of the Pullman-Peabody rolling stock ever developed. This was followed nine months later by the purchase of the designs and other assets of Philadelphia-based Transit America Inc., previously the mass transit equipment division of the Budd Company.

With these two acquisitions, Bombardier considerably strengthened its engineering resources and its ability to serve the North American market.

The 1982-1988 period closed with an agreement heralding a promising future in the mastery of new technologies. Having identified great potential for high-speed trains in North America, in December 1987 Bombardier signed a commercial and industrial cooperation agreement with Alsthom of France (now the French-British group GEC Alsthom) to promote and execute TGV (Train à Grande Vitesse) high-speed train projects in Canada and the United States.

*Mark VI monorail cars supplied by Bombardier
to Walt Disney World in Florida.*

Bombardier delivered 104 Horizon cars to Amtrak
following a 1988 order.

The TGV (Train à Grande Vitesse), the fastest train in the world,
has been operated in France for 10 years.

The first milestone
of European expansion

Even as it devoted major efforts and resources to reinforcing its North American position in the rail transportation equipment industry, Bombardier began exploring possibilities for overseas expansion as early as 1985. The prospect of a sizeable market in the united Europe of 1993 incited Bombardier to lay the foundation for European industrial expansion.

The opportunity arose when the Société Générale de Belgique was considering withdrawal from its minority stake in the Belgian manufacturer BN Constructions Ferroviaires et Métalliques s.a. Bombardier, which held a licence from BN for light rail vehicles since 1979, acquired 45% of the Belgian company's share capital in March 1986. This participation increased to 90.6% in 1988.

Besides widening Bombardier's scope of activity, this acquisition provided a new resource of technological expertise. In fact, BN is one of the European leaders in the design and construction of transportation equipment, and its important research and development capabilities have been applied to the development of advanced systems.

BN operates plants in various regions of Belgium. Its line of rolling stock includes standard and specialized boxcars, electric and diesel-electric locomotives, and a full line of rail transit vehicles. Highly active domestically, it had also enjoyed a number of successes on the international market. Vehicles built in its facilities are in service today in many countries.

Besides railway equipment, BN manufactures industrial products such as containers, aluminum truck bodies, industrial vehicles, and mechanical and mechanically welded components. This diverse activity allowed the company to withstand a temporary slowdown in the European transportation equipment market in 1987 and 1988. When the market recovered in 1989, major orders began to flow in again, and BN returned to its primary vocation.

BN's achievements over the last five years include a breakthrough in the British automatic tramway market and the development of a low-floor light rail vehicle, the LRV 2000. BN is also the leader of a Belgian consortium in the Cross-Channel Super Train project (a TGV to link Paris, Brussels and London via the English Channel tunnel).

BN is one of the major suppliers of the Belgian national railways.

*BN was a member of the Belgian consortium which built the
Manila light subway system in the Philippines.*

*London Regional Transport ordered a total of 70 automatic light
rail vehicles from BN for its Docklands line in London.*

Light rail vehicles delivered by BN to the Amsterdam transport authority in the Netherlands.

Launching into aerospace

Twelve years after diversifying into the transportation equipment business, Bombardier made another great stride by entering the field of aerospace. This became official when the Canadian government, which had decided to privatize Canadair some years earlier, accepted the Company's bid on December 23, 1986.

Established by the Canadian government in 1944, Canadair Limited was a subsidiary of the U.S. company General Dynamics Corporation for over 25 years. It returned to Canadian government ownership in 1976. When Canadair was privatized in 1986, it had built 4,000 civil and military aircraft, including 580 supersonic models.

The acquisition of Canadair fit perfectly with the dynamics of Bombardier's expansion, fulfilling the same criteria that had guided the Company's strategy for expansion into the transportation equipment field.

The Canadair purchase brought Bombardier a large pool of human resources and technical expertise which had been applied to develop in-house products, including the twin-engine Challenger* business jet, the CL-215* amphibious aircraft, and the CL-289* and CL-227* unmanned airborne surveillance systems. Moreover, Canadair held leading positions in these niche markets. Its components manufacturing activities represented an additional advantage, as they ensured ongoing relations with major American aircraft manufacturers such as Boeing and McDonnell Douglas. Canadair also had a long track record in supplying technical support services for various military aircraft which it had built.

A number of successes and new programs soon confirmed the wisdom of the Canadair purchase. Shortly after final agreement was reached, Bombardier signed a major contract to provide technical support for the Canadian Forces CF-18 fighters. The following month, the go-ahead was given on the development of a turboprop version of the CL-215 amphibian, and a first production order for the CL-289 surveillance system was received from Germany and France.

In 1988, the Challenger aircraft saw its share of the large business jet market rise by nearly 10%, and continued to account for the largest part of the sales volume in the Company's aerospace business segment.

Also in 1988, the French manufacturer Aerospatiale commissioned Canadair to design, develop and manufacture six major fuselage components for the A330 and A340 Airbus airliners. This first European supply contract was followed by a second from British Aerospace, which involved components for the same Airbus series. Meanwhile, in the North American aircraft component market, Canadair's order book was kept well filled by the renewal of existing contracts with Boeing and McDonnell Douglas.

And then in March 1989, Bombardier gave the green light to a new program which would mark a turning point in the Company's history: the Canadair Regional Jet* program, which called for the development of a 50-passenger jetliner for regional transportation. The aircraft was awarded Canadian Certification on July 31, 1992.

The signing of the letter of intent for the acquisition of Canadair, on August 18, 1986:
(rear) The Honourable Robert de Cotret, then President of the Treasury Board;
and The Honourable Marcel Masse, then Minister of Energy, Mines and Resources;
(front) Laurent Beaudoin, Chairman and Chief Executive Officer of Bombardier; and
The Honourable Barbara McDougall, then Minister of State for Privatization.

The 601-3A, which is the third generation of the twin-engine Challenger widebody business jet, was certificated in Canada and the United States in April 1987.

*The CL-215 amphibian is the only aircraft in the world designed
expressly for aerial firefighting. Canadair had delivered 124 CL-215 amphibians
to eight countries by the time this program ended in 1990.*

The CL-289 unmanned airborne surveillance system:
a rocket-launched drone capable of transmitting real-time images
and data to a ground station via computer link.

*Maintenance work on the Canadian Forces CF-18 fighter aircraft at a new facility
built near the Montréal International Airport (Mirabel).*

*Aircraft component manufacturing at Canadair's principal facility in the
Montréal suburb of Ville Saint-Laurent: (above) an aft fuselage pressure dome for the Boeing 767;
(below) a keel beam for the Airbus A330/A340 airliners built by Aerospatiale of France.*

*The 50-passenger Canadair Regional Jet is the only
twin-jet airliner of its kind on the market.*

The Olympic Games

While Bombardier was in full pursuit of its diversification goals, its tracked vehicles and snowmobiles came into the limelight when they took part in two Winter Olympics.

Both in Sarajevo, Yugoslavia in 1984 and in Calgary, Alberta in 1988, Bombardier was designated the exclusive official supplier of the tracked vehicles needed for the logistics of the Games.

At Sarajevo, the Austrian subsidiary Bombardier-Wien Schienenfahrzeuge AG[1] supplied 13 BR-1000* vehicles – huge tracked vehicles designed to groom the alpine, slalom and giant slalom runs. In addition, smaller vehicles built by the Industrial Equipment Division in Valcourt were used to groom the cross-country ski trails, and the Alpine utility model of the Ski-Doo snowmobile was used to provide all over-snow transportation, whether for judges, officials, rescue teams, course inspection or emergency services.

Four years later, Bombardier supplied a total of 87 vehicles to the organizing committee of the Calgary Winter Olympic Games. This fleet included BR-400* vehicles to groom the ski runs, BR-200* and SV-252* vehicles to maintain cross-country ski trails, as well as Safari* 503 and Alpine II snowmobiles to transport people and equipment.

In both cases, Bombardier provided teams of on-site specialists to drive and maintain the vehicles.

In Calgary, however, the Company's contribution began well before the official opening of the Games. A twin-engine Challenger business jet brought the Olympic flame from Greece to Canada in November 1987. This historic 10,000-kilometre trip began on November 11 when the Challenger took off from Calgary with senior officials of the Organizing Committee on board.

Having been flown from Olympia by relay, the flame was handed over to the Canadian delegation at an official ceremony in Athens. It was then flown from Athens to St. John's, Newfoundland, aboard the Challenger on November 18, to begin the relay which would carry it across Canada to Calgary.

A few months later, Bombardier also contributed three Safari 503 Ski-Doo snowmobiles for the Olympic Torch Relay. From January 7 to 18, 1988, the torch bearers used these vehicles to cross nearly 3,000 kilometres of snowbound land in Ontario, Manitoba and Saskatchewan.

Father Maurice Ouimet, the missionary who had received the very first Ski-Doo snowmobile from Joseph-Armand Bombardier, and who had dedicated his life to working with Native communities in the Far North, carried the torch for the first kilometre of this part of the trip. He was chosen for this honour to highlight his role as a pioneer in the history of the snowmobile.

(1) Previously Lohnerwerke GmbH.

The BR-1000 grooming vehicle at the Sarajevo Winter Olympics in 1984.

*Before and during the Calgary Winter Olympics in 1988,
the BR-400 demonstrated its endurance and performance.*

The team which travelled aboard a Challenger aircraft to bring the Olympic flame from Greece to Canada: (from top to bottom) Mr. Bill Pratt, President of O.C.O. (Olympiques Calgary Olympics); Mr. Ed Lakusta, President and Chief Operating Officer of Petro Canada Inc.; Dr. Roger Jackson, President of the Canadian Olympic Association and Dean of the Department of Physical Education of the University of Calgary; Mr. William J. Warren, Chairman of the Calgary Olympic Development Association; J.R. André Bombardier, Vice-Chairman of Bombardier; mascots (from left to right) Mr. Lane Kanenburg, Chairman of the Mascot Committee of O.C.O. and Mr. Larry Fisher (Hidy), Official Photographer of O.C.O.

Father Maurice Ouimet, of the Oblate order,
participated in the 1988 Olympic Torch Relay.
The snowmobile he used is now on display
at the J. Armand Bombardier Museum in Valcourt.

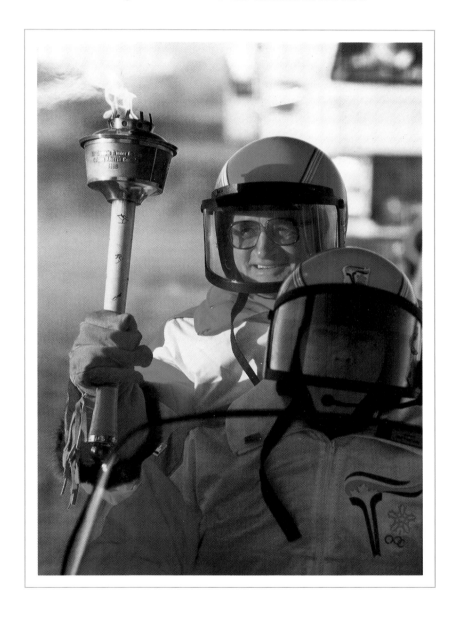

The Sea-Doo watercraft

The 1982-1988 period came to a close with the launch of the Sea-Doo watercraft, which was to ensure a greater presence for the Company in the recreational consumer goods market.

The decision to develop, manufacture and market the Sea-Doo watercraft was made after a careful exploration of the market potential for recreational marine products. The 1988 market launch of this new product was part of a strategy to strike a better balance between activities dependent on institutional markets and those related to consumer goods.

Bombardier had already developed an avant-garde watercraft design in 1968 and gone as far as to build and market that original vehicle under the Sea-Doo name. The concept was picked up again 20 years later, and the design was revised and improved to meet the demands of a promising new market.

The Sea-Doo was well received from the moment it hit the market in 1988 and earned the praise of two prestigious American consumer magazines. *Popular Science* listed it among the 100 most outstanding new products and technological advances of 1988 and declared it the winner in its category. *Popular Mechanics* ranked it the number one watercraft of its type on the market.

In the ensuing years Bombardier's newest creation continued to demonstrate its superiority and win bigger market shares, not only in North America, but also in Europe, Asia and Latin America.

Equipped with a safe and reliable high-performance product, Bombardier intends to carve out a choice position in this relatively young market.

*The 1968 Sea-Doo watercraft, at the Man and His World marina
in Montréal, before leaving on a 780-kilometre (460-mile) trip to New York.
It was the first vehicle of its kind to be built and marketed.*

*The Sea-Doo watercraft is a small personal craft that lends
itself as easily to sports performance as to recreation.
This is the first model of the new-generation Sea-Doo watercraft, launched in 1988.*

*A Sea-Doo dealer meeting at the Club Med Sandpiper Resort
in Florida, in 1991. Today, the Sea-Doo dealership network covers all of
North America and extends to 50 countries.*

International presence and Canadian expansion

In 1988, Bombardier was well on the way to achieving the goals it had set for itself. The undisputed North American leader of the rail transit industry and foremost airframe manufacturer in Canada, the Company also remained the world leader in snowmobiles and planned to carve out a choice position in the watercraft market.

In light of these achievements, the activities related to locomotive and diesel engine production were no longer in line with Bombardier's strategic goals, and a decision was made to exit this field. The assets and operations of the Rail and Diesel Products Division were therefore sold to General Electric of Canada (GE Canada) in 1989.

Concurrently with this consolidation, Bombardier pursued an ambitious international expansion program between 1988 and 1992 to secure its industrial presence in growing markets.

Beginning in 1988 with the affiliation of BN, of Belgium, international expansion into transportation equipment continued with the acquisition of the French company ANF-Industrie in 1989, the British firm Procor Engineering Limited in 1990, and the Mexican company Constructora Nacional de Carros de Ferrocarril s.a. in 1992. There was also expansion in aerospace, with the 1989 purchase of Short Brothers PLC in Northern Ireland, and the 1990 purchase of Learjet Corporation in the United States. In the snowmobile field, Bombardier formed a partnership with its Finnish distributor Starckjohann-Telko in 1988 for the acquisition of production facilities in Finland and Sweden.[1]

Having established a multinational presence on two continents, Bombardier also broadened its industrial base in Canada during this time with the purchase of two Ontario-based companies in 1992: railway equipment manufacturer UTDC and aircraft builder de Havilland.

Through this expansion program, the Company's size doubled in only four years.

(1) The Swedish plant closed in 1990.

In France...
and in England

About 20 months after becoming the majority shareholder of BN in Belgium, Bombardier took the next major step in its European development strategy when it finalized the purchase of ANF-Industrie, a French railway equipment manufacturer, in December 1989.

ANF-Industrie dates back to 1882, when a group of French and Belgian entrepreneurs founded Les Ateliers de construction du Nord de la France (A.N.F.) to produce transportation equipment for railway companies.

In 1970, A.N.F. became a holding company and transferred its railway equipment operations to a subsidiary named ANF-Industrie. Bombardier bought this subsidiary and gained a new pool of skills and a production facility in the heart of Western Europe, where the potential market for transportation equipment was then estimated to be four times greater than that in North America.

Today, ANF-Industrie is equipped to produce a wide range of railway products including diesel railcars, self-propelled electric vehicles for urban and commuter transit, mainline train cars, as well as non-motorized and motorized bogies (undercarriages). ANF-Industrie's subsidiary, Sofanor, makes seats and interior design elements for rolling stock.

In addition to being a national supplier, ANF-Industrie has developed a significant export business over the past two decades. The company participated in the construction of the Montréal, Mexico City, Santiago (Chile) and Caracas subway systems, and from 1982 to 1987, it was the leader of the Francorail group which provided 425 subway cars to New York City. During this same period, ANF-Industrie also produced 236 passenger railway cars for Iraq.

The French subsidiary's current production consists primarily of shuttle-train cars for the English Channel tunnel, pre-production units for the new generation of Paris subway cars, coaches and bogies for various TGV projects in France, and bi-level powered cars for the French national railways.

Once it was established in Belgium and France, Bombardier pursued its international expansion on the other side of the Channel. In October 1990, through its subsidiary BN, it bought all of the shares of Procor Engineering Limited, a British manufacturer of rail transport equipment located in Wakefield, England.

Now called Bombardier Prorail Limited, this company specializes in the production of body structures for locomotives and rail coaches, mainly for the United Kingdom market.

In May 1991, the activities of Bombardier's European transportation equipment subsidiaries were grouped under the name Bombardier Eurorail (Société anonyme). Already well-known in their respective markets, all of the units – Bombardier-Wien (Vienna), BN, ANF-Industrie and Bombardier Prorail – retained their own identities, own personnel and own operations.

For several years now, ANF-Industrie has been involved in the production
of bi-level cars for the commuter services of the French national railways (SNCF).

The turbotrain developed by ANF-Industrie in the 1970s
was sold to the SNCF as well as to the United States, Iran and Egypt.

The highly comfortable seats in the French TGV cars are
built by Sofanor, a subsidiary of ANF-Industrie.

In Northern Ireland

At the end of 1988, the integration of Canadair, which had been under way for two years, was going smoothly and already showing positive results. When the British government announced its decision to privatize the Short Brothers PLC (Shorts) aircraft manufacturer of Northern Ireland, Bombardier decided to seize the opportunity to reinforce its aerospace capabilities and establish a European presence in this industry.

Bombardier's purchase offer was accepted in June 1989 and Shorts became a wholly owned subsidiary of Bombardier when the agreement was finalized four months later.

Founded in 1901 by the Short brothers in Hove, England, and taken into government ownership in 1943, Shorts ranked among the pioneers of aviation. It received the first aircraft production contract from the Wright brothers in 1909, and an 80-year history of achievement followed. Over the years the company developed design and manufacturing technologies that contributed to the progress of aviation. It has a long line of civil and military aircraft and seaplanes to its credit.

Shorts, which moved to Belfast in 1937 and finally closed its English operation in 1947, is the biggest private company in Northern Ireland today.

In accordance with its corporate strategy, Bombardier evaluated both the strengths and weaknesses of Shorts before committing to buy, focusing on technological capabilities and the ability to penetrate global market niches.

At the time of the acquisition, Shorts already possessed advanced technology and a highly qualified workforce. The company had a well-filled order book and its vast experience in the regional aircraft market could be put to good use in the Canadair Regional Jet program.

Bombardier also took into account the difficult socio-economic climate that exists in Northern Ireland and chose to fully endorse Shorts' equal opportunity hiring policy.

Furthermore, Bombardier's acquisition brought with it a capital restructuring and a much needed investment program to modernize the plant, machinery and systems. Together with Shorts' own initiatives on total quality and organizational change, Bombardier's ownership was the catalyst for far-reaching changes resulting in increased employment and greatly improved financial performance.

Shorts is currently involved in the production of civil and military aircraft, the supply of components to major American and European aircraft manufacturers and the supply of nacelle systems and components to leading European engine makers, as well as the design and manufacture of close-air defence systems.

Signing of the Short Brothers PLC (Shorts) purchase agreement in Belfast, Northern Ireland, on October 4, 1989: (back) Roy McNulty, now President of Shorts; and David Haggan, then Chairman of the Shorts Factory Committee; (front) The Honourable Peter Brooke MP, Secretary of State for Northern Ireland; and Laurent Beaudoin, Chairman and Chief Executive Officer of Bombardier.

The Sherpa C-23 military transport is currently used by
the U.S. Air Force and the U.S. Army National Guard.*

The Shorts Tucano, the world's most advanced turboprop trainer,
has been in service with the U.K. Royal Air Force since 1989.*

Shorts is the European leader in the design and manufacture of jet-engine nacelles and nacelle components. Its clients for these products include Rolls Royce and British Aerospace.

As a partner in the Fokker 100 program, Shorts is responsible for the design and production of the complete wings of the aircraft.

*Shorts is a sole-source supplier of major components for
the Boeing 737, 747 and 757 airliners.*

*Shorts is a world leader in close-air defence
systems for protection against aircraft and helicopter attacks.*

*The centre fuselage section of the Regional Jet is built at
the Shorts facilities, and then sent to the Canadair assembly plant. Shorts also
produces the wing-mounted flight components for this aircraft.*

In the United States...
and in Mexico

Only a few months after the Shorts purchase, another transaction gave Bombardier access to the American aerospace industry, along with the most complete range of business jets on the market. This transaction involved the acquisition of the assets and operations of the Learjet Corporation, builder of the famous Learjet* aircraft.

The transaction was made through Learjet Inc., an American Bombardier subsidiary created for this purpose. It was completed on June 29, 1990, at the Learjet headquarters in Wichita, Kansas.

Learjet was named after its founder, the late William P. Lear Sr., who settled in Wichita in 1962 to develop a light jet geared to business travellers. The Learjet 23 was the first aircraft of its kind to be produced commercially, and it quickly earned an international reputation.

At the time of the purchase, the Learjet product range included three light models, the Learjet 31, 35A and 36A, as well as the medium-sized Learjet 55C. Combined with the widebody Canadair Challenger twin-engine jet, this product range ensured a leading place for Bombardier in the business aircraft market.

Like Canadair and Shorts, Learjet is also a subcontractor for a number of other aerospace concerns. Its current clients include the U.S. Air Force, Boeing and Martin Marietta Manned Space Systems.

In addition to its headquarters, all of Learjet's production facilities and an after-sales service centre are located in Wichita. Another service and completion centre for both Learjet and Canadair Challenger aircraft is based in Tucson, Arizona. A network of affiliated aircraft maintenance centres spread throughout the United States and abroad serves the large fleet of Learjet aircraft currently in operation.

Following the purchase, Bombardier granted financial support to two product development projects, the Learjet 31A and the Learjet 60, aimed at improving Learjet's competitive position in the market.

In June 1990, the go-ahead was given to construct a new flight testing and development facility on the Learjet premises in Wichita. The centre, which began operating in the summer of 1991, is being used in the development of new Learjet and Canadair products. It is one example of the multiple synergies flowing from the expansion of Bombardier's activities.

In May 1992, as part of its ongoing expansion program, Bombardier completed the acquisition of a Mexican company, Constructora Nacional de Carros de Ferrocarril S.A., commonly referred to as Concarril.

Created by the Mexican government in 1954, Concarril, now operated under the name of Bombardier S.A. de C.V., is Mexico's leading manufacturer of railway rolling stock. Located in Ciudad Sahagun in the Mexico City region, the Concarril facilities are equipped to produce a full range of rail transit vehicles, including rubber-tired and steel-wheeled subway cars, light rail vehicles, passenger coaches and freight cars.

This acquisition opens up new markets for Bombardier, not only in Mexico, but in other Latin American countries and in the Southern United States.

*The Learjet 31A, an improved version of the light Learjet 31,
obtained U.S. certification in July 1991.*

*The Learjet 60, a new arrival in the Learjet line of business
aircraft, completed its inaugural flight in June 1991.*

*As a sub-contractor for the Manned Space Systems Division of
Martin Marietta of the U.S., Learjet manufactures
crucial components of the Space Shuttle's external fuel tank.*

The first of the three aircraft used for the Canadair Regional Jet
flight test and certification program arrived in Wichita on July 16, 1991.

The Learjet service centre in Tucson provides after-sale service, completion
and refurbishment for Challenger aircraft operating in the Western United States.

And in Canada

In early 1992, Bombardier signed two purchase agreements which enabled it to establish an industrial base in Ontario in each of its two main fields of activity.

In February, the Company finalized the acquisition of the Canadian rail transit assets of UTDC Inc., a manufacturer of rail transport equipment.

This new Bombardier unit was created by the Ontario government in 1973 to design, develop, market and deliver urban transit equipment, and to act as a catalyst for the development of products at the leading edge of transportation technology.

To fulfill its mandate, UTDC first built a testing track, along with research and development facilities, in Kingston, Ontario, adding a manufacturing plant in 1982. Two years later, UTDC bought Hawker Siddeley's Canadian Car plant in Thunder Bay, Ontario.

In 1975, UTDC began researching an automated light rail transit system which it later built and marketed. The range of UTDC equipment includes light rail vehicles, subway cars and commuter rail cars.

Between 1982 and 1992, UTDC manufactured nearly 800 rail transit vehicles for a number of North American authorities including those of Boston, Detroit, Los Angeles, New York, Toronto and Vancouver.

Bombardier finalized the purchase of Boeing's de Havilland division in March 1992, through de Havilland Inc., a newly created company, whose equity is shared by Bombardier (51%) and the Province of Ontario (49%).

Founded in 1928 in Downsview, Ontario, to assemble and sell the products of its British parent company, de Havilland Canada has since built some 7,000 aircraft.

In the 1950s, after its wartime production had ended and the Beaver* – created for bush operations – had been perfected, de Havilland began to make its mark in STOL (short take-off and landing) aircraft.

During the next two decades, the Downsview-based manufacturer ushered in the era of regional air transport with the introduction of two turboprop aircraft: the Twin Otter*, launched in the 1960s under Hawker Siddeley, and the Dash* 7 airliner, launched in the 1970s after the company was bought by the Canadian government.

Today, de Havilland offers the Dash 8 family of aircraft, the first of the new-generation regional airliners to be developed in the 1980s. The combination of the de Havilland Dash 8 turboprop aircraft and the Canadair Regional Jet establishes Bombardier as one of the world leaders in the regional aircraft market.

Signing of the agreement in principle for Bombardier's acquisition of the Canadian mass transit assets of Ontario-based UTDC, on December 10, 1991: (left) Mr. Gilles Pouliot, Ontario Minister of Transport; and (right) Raymond Royer, Bombardier President and Chief Operating Officer.

The SkyTrain Advanced Light Rail Transit system was delivered to Vancouver by UTDC for the Transpo '86 world's fair.

Aluminum subway cars built at the UTDC Thunder Bay plant for Toronto.

Light rail vehicles built by UTDC for Santa Clara County, California.
Some 250 light rail vehicles were also delivered to the Toronto Transit Commission.

The bi-level commuter rail coaches built by UTDC for
Toronto's GO-Train system are the largest of their kind in the world.
Each can accommodate up to 400 passengers.

The signing of the agreement in principle for the purchase of Ontario-based manufacturer de Havilland: (left to right) The Honourable Ed Philip, Ontario Minister for Industry, Trade and Technology; Laurent Beaudoin, Chairman and Chief Executive Officer of Bombardier; The Honourable Bob Rae, Premier of Ontario; Mr. Jim O'Neil, National Secretary/Treasurer, Canadian Auto Workers; and The Honourable Michael Wilson, Canadian Minister for Industry, Science and Technology, and Minister for International Trade.

The Dash 8 Series 100 turboprop regional aircraft, with a 37-40 passenger capacity, has enjoyed great market success since introduction to service in 1984.

The Dash 8 Series 300 was launched in 1986 after Boeing's acquisition of de Havilland Canada. This aircraft, with a 50-56 passenger capacity, was certificated in 1989.

Today's great projects

Even as Bombardier consolidates its recent acquisitions, it remains alert to new opportunities that fit the focus and goals of its mission statement.

In the field of motorized consumer products, maintaining a leadership position requires continued improvement of the quality and performance of the Ski-Doo snowmobiles and Sea-Doo watercraft, as well as a well-defined and aggressive marketing strategy geared to consumer expectations.

Bombardier, which has manufactured over two million Ski-Doo snowmobiles since 1959, today offers a wide range of models. The 1992 series represents a major milestone in the product's evolution, as the first of a new generation of sporting snowmobiles at the leading edge of technology.

In the same way, Bombardier intends to maintain the Sea-Doo watercraft's superiority, which has been recognized since the product was introduced in 1988. The development of increasingly safe and powerful models will allow Bombardier to efficiently maintain its competitiveness in a market niche that has become globalized within a few short years.

Major projects set in motion over the last few years are intended to ensure the immediate and long-term future of the Company's other activities.

In rail transit equipment, the future depends in part on the Company's ability to anticipate trends and adapt to the needs of its customers into the next century.

A project begun in 1990 demonstrates this very ability. It calls for Bombardier to develop, build, and test new-generation subway car prototypes for the New York City Transit Authority (NYCTA), the largest urban transit authority in the United States.

Also in 1990, Bombardier and GEC Alsthom began promoting a TGV high-speed train system for the Quebec City–Windsor corridor. This project is considered a solid base from which to market the TGV throughout North America, where more than 20 corridors display the appropriate market characteristics for such a system.

In Europe, French subsidiary ANF-Industrie is also preparing for the future with the development and production of pre-production units for the next generation of Paris subway cars.

Internationally, Bombardier has drawn prestige from its participation in one of the great technical and financial projects of the century, the English Channel tunnel. The Company is the only North American member of the Euroshuttle Consortium, which was chosen in 1989 to produce the shuttle trains that will transport automobiles and buses through the tunnel. Acting as the production leader for the enormous wagons, Bombardier is carrying out this contract through its Transportation Equipment Group – North America, and BN and ANF-Industrie in Europe. The Group is responsible for designing the car bodies and manufacturing the stainless steel sub-assemblies. The European units are responsible for systems design and final assembly of the single-deck bus-carrying wagons (BN) and the double-deck automobile-carrying ones (ANF-Industrie).

In defence, where research and development activities are intimately tied to the growth capacity of companies, the development of the CL-227 unmanned airborne surveillance system at Canadair and the high-velocity Starstreak* close-air defence system at Shorts should allow Bombardier to maintain its lead in two highly specialized market niches with good prospects.

Bombardier's reading of aviation market trends has resulted in the 1991 launch of the Global Express* project, which involves developing a new world-class business jet. The proposed aircraft would extend the Bombardier range of business jets and provide the utmost degree of service and comfort to business executives, who will be called upon to travel faster and further than ever before in order to conduct business in the increasingly "global" context of the twenty-first century.

The Company has also taken a prominent role in the amphibian aircraft segment by developing the CL-415*. This turboprop aircraft takes over from the CL-215, which has a quarter-century tradition of fighting forest fires. Production of the CL-415 began in October 1991, following an order for 12 units awarded by the French government. The new aircraft incorporates many innovative features that provide increased efficiency in its fire-fighting role.

In 1989, Bombardier made a full-fledged entry into the airliner industry when it launched the Canadair Regional Jet, a 50-passenger aircraft that will enable air carriers to increase the frequency of their regional flights and serve outlying destinations while providing better passenger comfort. The Regional Jet currently has no competitors in its category. This gives Bombardier a substantial advantage in the regional commercial aviation market, where potential demand for this kind of aircraft is estimated at 1,200 for the 1990s.

The cockpit of the new high-performance Formula MXZ model,
which includes Nightdial Instrumentation with a backlit speedometer, illustrates
the advanced features of the new generation of Ski-Doo snowmobiles.*

The powerful and luxurious GTX model, introduced in 1992,
is the top of the Sea-Doo watercraft line.*

*The CL-227 Sentinel unmanned airborne surveillance system participated
in NATO exercises in the North Atlantic as part of an operational demonstration program
on board the American frigate USS Doyle.*

*The high-velocity Starstreak missile was designed to meet the
British Army's requirements for close-air defence systems in the twenty-first century.*

*The nine prototype subway cars which Bombardier designed
for the NYCTA use high-technology components.*

*Bombardier, BN and ANF-Industrie are working together to build
shuttle train cars for the English Channel tunnel.*

*A trainset of pre-production units, designed and built by ANF-Industrie
for the next generation of Paris subway cars.*

*The Canadian TGV, proposed by Bombardier and GEC Alsthom
for a high-speed passenger rail link in the Quebec City–Windsor corridor.
In Texas, the two companies have been chosen as rolling stock suppliers
for a TGV project which is at the financing stage.*

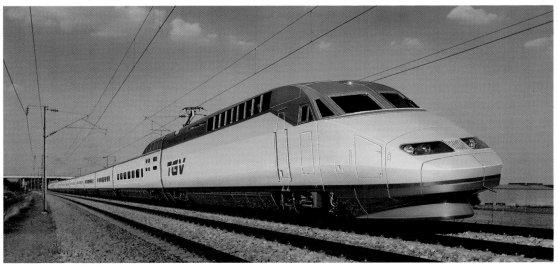

Thanks to its spacious three-compartment cabin, identical in length to that of the Regional Jet, Canadair's proposed Global Express aircraft would make long 12-hour flights productive and restful for business and government leaders.

The CL-415 turboprop amphibious aircraft built by Canadair for France

The rollout of the Regional Jet on May 6, 1991 was a memorable event
attended by Canadair employees and many key figures from
the aerospace and commercial aviation world.
Only four days later, the Regional Jet made its inaugural flight.

Tomorrow's challenges

The organization has come a long way in the half-century since the incorporation of L'Auto-Neige Bombardier in 1942.

While entrepreneur and inventor Joseph-Armand Bombardier created his company to build tracked vehicles, today Bombardier Inc. is one of Canada's largest manufacturing companies, with a variety of goods and services in four major sectors: motorized consumer products, transportation equipment, aerospace and defence.

A sales volume that totalled $211,800 in 1942-43 has increased tenfold and a hundredfold to reach $3 billion in 1991-92.

Based in Québec's Eastern Townships for nearly 30 years, Bombardier's industrial activity has extended far beyond Canada's borders in the last two decades, spreading to the United States, Mexico, Austria, Belgium, the United Kingdom, France and Finland, to achieve international scope.

While L'Auto-Neige Bombardier found its clientele in the snowbound regions of North America, Bombardier now serves customers in many different markets on five continents, and more than 90% of its sales are made outside Canada.

Throughout its evolution, Bombardier has targeted specialized niche markets with good growth potential. The result is a company well poised for the future, with prime positions in each of its markets. Thus, Bombardier offers world markets a wide range of vehicles for urban, commuter and intercity rail transit. The only manufacturer with a full line of business jets, the Company is also making headway in the regional air transport niche and ranks among the world's foremost specialists in airborne surveillance and close-air defence systems. In addition to having a leadership position in the snowmobile industry, it is well placed in the watercraft market with a product that is enjoying the highest sales growth rate in its category. As to the financing subsidiaries, they now provide their services to a wide range of durable consumer goods industries. Finally, Bombardier Immobilier Ltée, a subsidiary created in 1990, is responsible for developing the Company's real estate assets.

This is the solid foundation upon which Bombardier can rely as it faces the challenges of globalizing markets.

Bombardier's future depends to a great extent on the talent and dedication of some 32,000 men and women who make up the Bombardier team. This page is meant as a tribute to those who have contributed to the Company's success over the past 50 years, and as an encouragement to new employees taking on their first challenges.